W9-DDJ-017

Mirtha Toledo
Aug. 14, 2,000
Valparaiso, IN

CONFUCIUS
The WISDOM

Sincerity is the way of Heaven.

— CONFUCIUS

THIS BOOK WAS GIVEN TO

Mirtha

BY

Mirtha

ON

Aug. 14, 2,000

WATERCOLORS BY
Claudia Karabaic Sargent

SELECTED AND EDITED BY
Peg Streep

FROM THE TRANSLATION BY
James Legge

CONFUCIUS
The WISDOM

A BULFINCH PRESS BOOK
LITTLE, BROWN AND COMPANY
Boston   New York   Toronto   London

*For Mitch, who always believed in the work,
and in me.*

— C.K.S.

FIRST EDITION

LIBRARY OF CONGRESS CATALOGING-IN-PUBLICATION DATA

Confucius : the wisdom / watercolors by Claudia Karabaic Sargent ;
selected and edited by Peg Streep, from the translation by James
Legge. — 1st ed.
p.   cm.
ISBN 0-8212-2161-2
1. Confucius — Quotations. I. Sargent, Claudia Karabaic. II. Streep,
Peg. III. Legge, James, 1815–1897.
B128.C8C58 1995
181'. 112 — dc20

94-41432

*Bulfinch Press is an imprint and trademark of
Little, Brown and Company (Inc.)*

*Published simultaneously in Canada by
Little, Brown & Company (Canada) Limited*

PRINTED IN ITALY

INTRODUCTION

*T*he importance of the legacy of *K'ung Fu-tse,* or
Confucius, as we know him in the West, to the culture
of the world's most populous country can hardly be
overstated. For some two thousand years, the words of
the works traditionally ascribed to Confucius have been
memorized by generation after generation of Chinese;
probably the only work with equivalent cultural
importance in the West is the Bible.

Little is known about the historical Confucius, and
separating the truth about the man from the many
legends that grew up around him is difficult indeed.
We know that he was born sometime around 551 B.C.
and that he died in approximately 479 B.C., although
the works from which the text of this book is drawn —
The Analects, The Great Learning, and *The Doctrine of*
the Mean — were compiled after his death. What details
we have about Confucius' life are gleaned from the
Lun yi or "Selected Sayings," commonly known in the
West as *The Analects.* Born in the state of Lu, now in
the modern province of Shantung, to a noble but poor
family, Confucius devoted himself to learning at the age
of fifteen. He subsequently became a teacher and then,
in his thirties, held various state jobs only to leave Lu
after an upheaval in the government. When he returned
to Lu at the age of fifty, he again held several posts,
among them police commissioner of the province. We
do not know why Confucius left Lu somewhat precipi-
tously (the accounts vary), but we do know that he
spent thirteen years traveling throughout the various
feudal states that then comprised China. Disturbed by
the constant warfare and bloodshed among these states
and the tyrannical practices of the feudal rulers,
Confucius sought to have himself appointed to a post

so that he could put his philosophy into practice. Finally unsuccessful in his efforts (after apparently surviving an assassination attempt in the province of Sung), he returned to Lu five years before his death to devote his time to teaching his disciples. Many of the chapters in *The Analects* record the process of his teaching, as well as the achievements and shortcomings of his followers.

Confucius' philosophy was formulated in response to his political present; his was not wisdom for its own sake but rather a primer for the achievement of political goals. Hence, the *tao* or "Way" that appears in Confucius is not the mystical and sometimes contradictory *tao* of the *Tao te Ching* but a path to be followed by the application of knowledge, thought, and love. It is in this context that we must understand Confucius' emphasis on humane behavior or benevolence, on character, and on virtue, first in the individual and then in the ever-widening circle of relationships that comprise the personal sphere (parents, family, friends, neighbors) and that finally culminate in the largest sphere, the political entity of the state. These themes echo throughout the works; as here, from *The Doctrine of the Mean:*

> Benevolence is the characteristic element of humanity, and the great exercise of it is in loving relatives. Righteousness is the accordance of actions with what is right, and the great exercise of it is in honoring the worthy. The degrees of love due to relatives and steps in the honor due to the worthy are produced by the principles of propriety.

"Propriety," which encompasses ritual, custom, and the appropriate, is the great regulator of all benevo-

lence, righteousness, and moral behavior. And in the words of *The Analects*,

> Tsze-kung asked, saying, "Is there one word which may serve as a rule of practice for all one's life?"
> The Master said, "Is not *reciprocity* such a word? What you do not want done to yourself, do not do to others."

The Confucius who emerges from *The Analects* is not a philosopher born with wisdom or gifted with a higher degree of knowledge but, instead, a seeker of truth, demanding of himself and his students. His words remind us, again and again, to ignore the surface of life — the glib word, the specious argument, knowledge without understanding, the lure of salary — and to look within and nourish our humanity instead:

> The Master said, "With coarse rice to eat, with water to drink, and my bended arm for a pillow: I still have joy in the midst of these things. Riches and honors acquired by unrighteousness are as a floating cloud to me.

This collection has been organized into chapters — "Knowledge," "Virtue," "Character," and "Conduct" — although the selections make clear that these subjects, in Confucius' vision, are intimately connected. "Reciprocity" is the word that governs the Confucian universe. The translation from which I have worked is that of James Legge; the watercolors that embellish these pages have been inspired by centuries of Chinese art and have been especially created for this volume.

— PEG STREEP

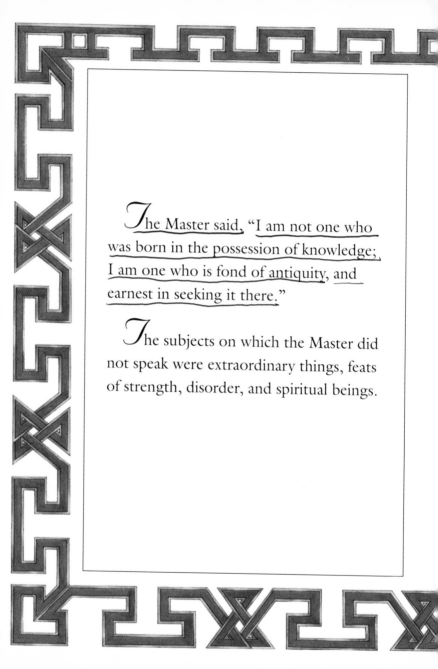

The Master said, "I am not one who was born in the possession of knowledge; I am one who is fond of antiquity, and earnest in seeking it there."

The subjects on which the Master did not speak were extraordinary things, feats of strength, disorder, and spiritual beings.

KNOWLEDGE

The Master said, "The pursuit of learning may be compared to what may happen in raising a mound. If there lacks but one basket of earth to complete the work, and I stop, the stopping is my own work. It may be compared to throwing down the earth on level ground. Even though only one basketful is thrown at a time, advancing with it is my own going forward."

The Master said, "By extensively studying all learning, and keeping oneself under the restraint of the rules of propriety, one may thus likewise not err from what is right."

The Master said, "A transmitter and not a maker, believing in and loving the ancients, I venture to compare myself with our old P'ang."

The Master said, "The silent treasuring up of knowledge, learning without satiety, and instructing others without being wearied—these things belong to me."

The Master said, "Leaving virtue without proper cultivation; not thoroughly discussing what is learned; not being able to move towards what is right; and not being able to change what is not good — these things cause me concern."

*W*hat the Great Learning teaches is to make virtue clear; to renovate the people; and to rest in the highest good.

The point of highest good being known, the object of pursuit is determined and, that being determined, a calm unperturbedness may be attained. To that calmness will succeed a tranquil repose. In that repose there may be careful deliberation and only after deliberation will the desired end be attained.

Things have their root and their branches. Affairs have their end and their beginning. To know what is first and what is last will lead to what is taught in the Great Learning.

The ancients who wished to make virtue clear throughout the kingdom first ordered well their own States. Wishing to order their States, they first regulated their families. Wishing to regulate their families, they first cultivated their persons. Wishing to cultivate their persons, they first rectified their hearts. Wishing to rectify their hearts, they first sought to be sincere in their thoughts. Wishing to be sincere in their thoughts, they first extended their knowledge to the *tell the truth* utmost limit. Such extension of knowledge lay in the investigation of things. *learning*

Things being investigated, knowledge became complete. Their knowledge being complete, their thoughts were sincere. Their thoughts being sincere, their hearts were then rectified. Their hearts being rectified, their persons were cultivated. Their persons being cultivated, their families were regulated. Their families being regulated, their States were rightly governed. Their States being rightly governed, the whole kingdom was made tranquil and happy. *it's a chain*

From the Son of Heaven down to the mass of the people, all must consider the cultivation of the person the root of everything besides.

When the root is neglected, that which springs from it cannot be ordered. It has never been the case that what was of great importance has been slightly cared for, and, at the same time that what was of slight importance has been greatly cared for.

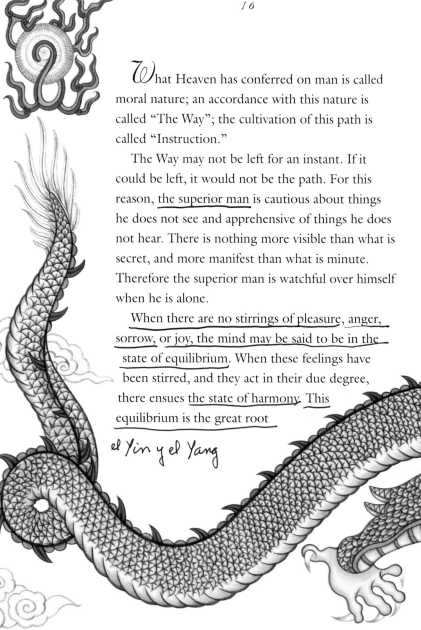

What Heaven has conferred on man is called moral nature; an accordance with this nature is called "The Way"; the cultivation of this path is called "Instruction."

The Way may not be left for an instant. If it could be left, it would not be the path. For this reason, the superior man is cautious about things he does not see and apprehensive of things he does not hear. There is nothing more visible than what is secret, and more manifest than what is minute. Therefore the superior man is watchful over himself when he is alone.

When there are no stirrings of pleasure, anger, sorrow, or joy, the mind may be said to be in the state of equilibrium. When these feelings have been stirred, and they act in their due degree, there ensues the state of harmony. This equilibrium is the great root

el Yin y el Yang

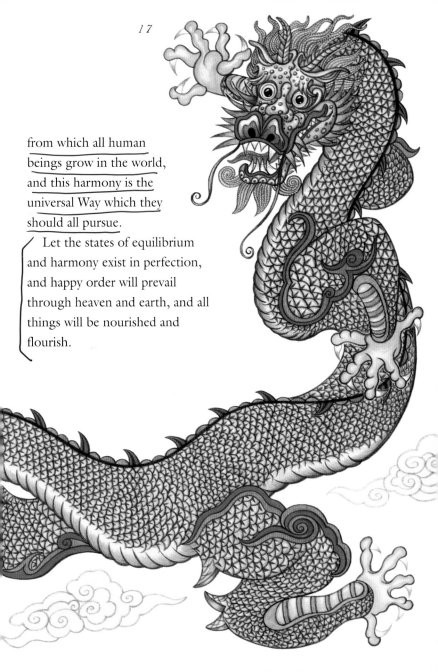

from which all human beings grow in the world, and this harmony is the universal Way which they should all pursue.

Let the states of equilibrium and harmony exist in perfection, and happy order will prevail through heaven and earth, and all things will be nourished and flourish.

The Master said, "Specious words confound virtue. Want of forbearance in small matters confounds great plans."

The Master said, "When the multitude dislike a man, it is necessary to examine into the case. When the multitude like a man, it is necessary to examine into the case."

The Master said, "A man can enlarge the Way which he follows; the Way does not enlarge the man."

The Way is

The Master said, "To have faults and not to reform them, this indeed should be pronounced having faults."

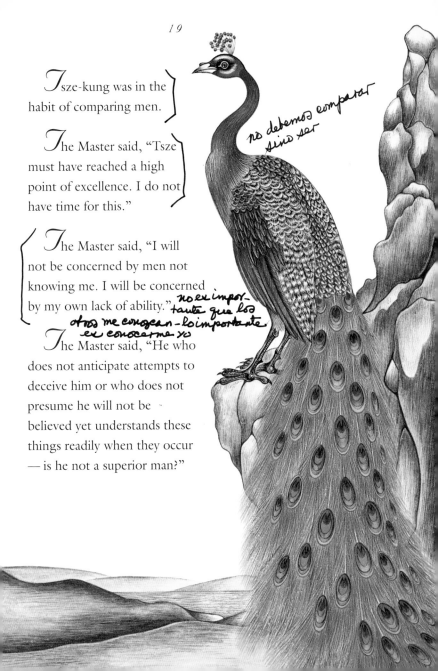

*T*sze-kung was in the habit of comparing men.

no debemos comparar sino ser

*T*he Master said, "Tsze must have reached a high point of excellence. I do not have time for this."

*T*he Master said, "I will not be concerned by men not knowing me. I will be concerned by my own lack of ability."

no es importante que los otros me conozcan - lo importante es conocerme yo

*T*he Master said, "He who does not anticipate attempts to deceive him or who does not presume he will not be believed yet understands these things readily when they occur — is he not a superior man?"

The Master said, "I have spent the whole day without eating, and the whole night without sleeping, occupied with thinking. It was of no use. The better plan is to learn." *pensar no es suficiente - hay que aprender y educarse*

The Master said, "The object of the superior man is truth, not food. Even in farming there is sometimes famine. So with learning, compensation may be found in it. The superior man is anxious lest he should not get truth; he is not anxious lest poverty should come upon him."

La Verdad, es ; tan esencial !

The Master said, "When a man's knowledge is sufficient to attain but his virtue is not sufficient to enable him to hold whatever he may have gained, he will lose again." *la virtud es superior al conocimiento ser hombre de bien*

"When his knowledge is sufficient to attain and his virtue enough to hold fast, if he cannot govern with dignity, the people will not respect him." *aún teniendo virtud y conocimiento, hace falta la dignidad*

"When his knowledge is sufficient to attain, when he has virtue enough to hold fast, and when he governs also with dignity, yet if he try to move the people contrary to the rules of propriety, full excellence is not reached." *aún teniendo todo lo anterior, también hace falta seguir las reglas de lo que es apropiado, la civilidad, lo correcto, la urbanidad*

The Master said, "The Way is not far from man. When men try to pursue a course and wish to be far from men, this course cannot be considered the Way."

¿ por qué ?

The Master said, "Yu, shall I teach you what knowledge is? When you know a thing, to hold that you know it; and when you do not know a thing, to allow that you do not know it — this is knowledge." ¡ claro ! saber la diferencia

$\mathcal{T}$sze-chang asked what constituted intelligence.

$\mathcal{T}$he Master said, "He with whom neither slander that gradually soaks into the mind nor statements that startle like a wound in the flesh are successful may be called intelligent indeed. Yes, he with whom neither soaking slander nor startling statements are successful may be called far-seeing." *el que está por encima de todo esto, es inteligente*

$\mathcal{T}$he Master said, "Learn as if you could not reach your object, and were always afraid lest you should lose it." *o sea, siempre*

The Master said, "I cannot see a sage; could I see a man of real talent and virtue, that would satisfy me."

The Master said, "A good man is not mine to see; could I see a man possessed of constancy, that would satisfy me."

Having not and yet affecting to have; empty yet affecting to be full; straitened and yet affecting to be at ease — it is difficult with such characteristics to have constancy.

The Master fished, but did not use a net. He shot, but not at birds perching.

The Master said, "There may be those who act without knowing why, but I do not do so. Hearing much and selecting what is good and following it, and seeing much and keeping it in memory — this is the second style of knowledge."

*F*an Ch'ih asked about benevolence.

The Master said, "It is to love *all* men."

He asked about knowledge.

The Master said, "It is to know *all* men."

Fan Ch'ih did not immediately understand these answers.

The Master said, "Employ the upright and put aside all the crooked; in this way, the crooked can be made to be upright."

Sincerity is the way of Heaven. The attainment of sincerity is the Way of men. He who possesses sincerity is he who hits what is right and apprehends, without the exercise of thought. He is the sage who naturally and easily embodies the Way. He who attains to sincerity is he who chooses what is good and firmly holds it fast.

To this attainment, the extensive study of what is good, accurate inquiry about it, careful reflection on it, the clear discrimination of it, and the earnest practice of it are requisite.

The superior man will not stop if there is anything he has not studied, or if there is

anything in what he has studied he cannot understand. He will not stop if there is anything he has not inquired about, or anything he does not know in what he has inquired about. He will not stop if there is anything he has not reflected on, or if he does not understand anything in what he has reflected on. He will not stop if there is anything he has not discerned, or if his discernment is not clear. He will not stop if there be anything he has not practiced, or his practice falls short in earnestness. If another man succeed by one effort, he will use a hundred efforts. If another man succeed by ten efforts, he will use a thousand.

Let man proceed in this way, and, though dull, he will surely become intelligent; though weak, he will surely become strong.

el secreto es continuar y no
desfallecer - superarse - seguir
más allá de lo que el hombre
regular, la masa, llega

Tsze-hsia said, "If a man withdraws his mind from the love of beauty, and applies it as sincerely to the love of the virtuous; if, in serving his parents, he uses all his energy; if, in serving his prince, he can devote his life; if, in his dealings with friends, his words are sincere: although men may say he has not learned, I would say that he has."

The Master said, "If the scholar is not grave, he will not gain respect, and his learning will not be solid."

"Hold faithfulness and sincerity as the first principles."

"Have no friends not equal to yourself. When you have faults, do not fear to abandon them."

The Master said, "When the year becomes cold, then we know that the pine and the cypress are the last to lose their leaves." *lo que es verdadero y fuerte no muere*

The Master said, "The wise are free from perplexities; the virtuous from anxiety; and the bold from fear." *para llegar aquí hay que ser un sabio como Confucio*

The Master said, "There are some with whom we may study in common, but it may not be possible to go on to the Way with them. Perhaps we may go on with them to the Way, but we may find them unable to get established in it along with us. Or if we do get so established with them, we should find them unable to weigh events along with us." *cierto*

The Master said, "Yu, have you heard the six words to which are attached six obfuscations?"

Yu replied, "I have not."

"Sit down," said the Master, "and I will tell them to you. There is the love of being benevolent without the love of learning: the obfuscation leads to foolishness. There is the love of knowing without the love of learning: the obfuscation here leads to lack of principle. There is the love of being sincere without the love of learning: the obfuscation here leads to an injurious disregard of consequences. There is the love of straightforwardness without the love of learning: the obfuscation here leads to rudeness. There is the love of boldness without the love of learning: the obfuscation here leads to insubordination. There is the love of firmness without the love of learning: the obfuscation here leads to recklessness."

lo importante en todo lo que se lege es: "the love of learning"

The Master said, "I would prefer not speaking."

Tsze-kung said, "If you, Master, do not speak, what shall we, your disciples, have to record?"

The Master said, "Does Heaven speak? The four seasons pursue their courses, and all things are continually being produced, but does Heaven say anything?" *Las acciones cuentan más que las palabras*

*A*ll things are nourished together without their injuring one another. The courses of the seasons and of the sun and moon are pursued without any collision among them. The smaller energies are like river currents; the greater energies are seen in mighty transformations. It is this which makes heaven and earth so good.

It is only he, possessed of all the sagely qualities that can exist under heaven, who shows himself quick in apprehension, clear in discernment, of far-reaching intelligence, and all-embracing knowledge, fitted to exercise rule; magnanimous, generous, benign, and mild, fitted to exercise forbearance; impulsive,

energetic, firm, and enduring; fitted to
maintain a firm hold; self-adjusted, grave,
never swerving from the Mean, and correct,
fitted to commend reverence; accomplished,
distinctive, concentrative and searching,
fitted to exercise discrimination.

All-embracing is he and vast, deep and
active as a fountain, sending forth his virtues
in due season.

All-embracing and vast is he like heaven.
Deep and active as a fountain; he is like the
abyss. He is seen, and the people all revere
him; he speaks, and the people believe him;
he acts, and the people all are pleased
with him.

Esta persona descrita aquí
se parece, en las cualidades,
a mami, aunque en el primer
párrafo, esa persona soy yo

las categorías de Confucio— los igno-rantes para él eran lo último

Confucius said, "Those who are born with the possession of knowledge are the highest class of men. Those who learn and readily attain knowledge are the next. Those who are dull and stupid, and yet encompass learning, are another class next to these. As to those who are dull and stupid and do not learn, they are the lowest of people."

Confucius said, "The superior man has nine things he considers thoughtfully: to see clearly when he uses his eyes; to hear distinctly when he uses his ears; to look benign; to be respectful in his demeanor; to be sincere in his speech; to be reverent in his doing business; to ask advice when he has doubts; to think of consequences when he is angry; to think of righteousness when he sees gain to be gotten."

Confucius said, "Contemplating good and pursuing it as if they could not reach it; contemplating evil and shrinking from it, as they would from thrusting their hands into boiling water — I have seen such men, as I have heard such words.

"Living in retirement to study their aims, and practicing righteousness to carry out their principles — I have heard those words, but I have not seen such men."

The Master said, "I do not open up the truth to one who is not eager to get knowledge, nor help out any-one who is not anxious to explain himself. When I have presented one corner of a square to anyone, and he cannot from it learn the other three, I do not repeat my lesson."

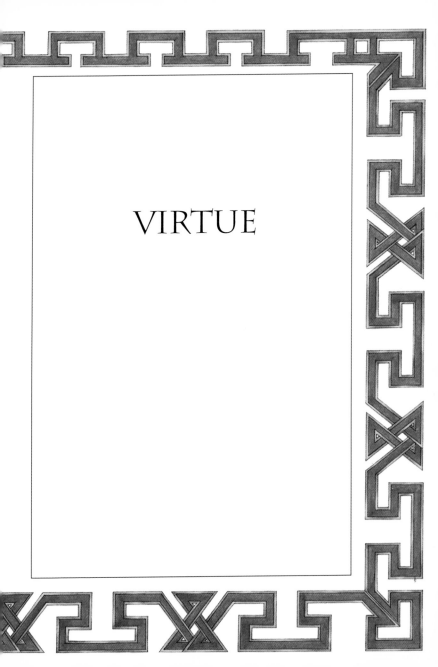

VIRTUE

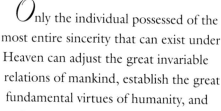

*O*nly the individual possessed of the most entire sincerity that can exist under Heaven can adjust the great invariable relations of mankind, establish the great fundamental virtues of humanity, and know the transforming and nurturing operations of Heaven and Earth.

Does this individual depend on any being or anything beyond himself? Call him man in his ideal; how earnest is he! Call him an abyss; how deep is he! Call him Heaven; how vast is he!

Who can know him, except he who is indeed quick in apprehension, clear in discernment, of far-reaching intelligence, and all-embracing knowledge, possessing all heavenly virtue?

The Master said, "The superior man cannot be known in small matters, but he may be entrusted with great concerns. The inferior man may not be entrusted with great concerns, but he may be known in little matters."

The Master said, "Virtue is more to man than either water or fire. I have seen men die from treading on water and fire but I have never seen a man die from treading the course of virtue."

The Master said, "Let every man consider virtue as what devolves on himself. He may not yield the performance of it even to his teacher."

The Master said, "The superior man is correctly firm and not firm merely."

The Master said, "A minister, in serving his prince, reverently discharges his duties and makes his pay a secondary consideration."

*H*ow great is the Way proper to the Sage! Like overflowing water, it sends forth and nourishes all things, and rises up to the height of heaven.

All complete is its greatness! It embraces the three hundred rules of ceremony, and the three thousand rules of demeanor.

It waits for the proper man, and then it is trodden.

Hence it is said, "Only by perfect virtue can the perfect Way, in all its courses, be made fact."

Therefore, the superior man honors his virtuous nature, and maintains constant inquiry and study, seeking to carry it out to its breadth and greatness, so as to omit none of the more exquisite and minute points which it embraces, and to raise it to its greatest height and brilliancy, so as to pursue the path of the Mean. He cherishes his old knowledge, and is continually acquiring new. He exerts an honest, generous earnestness, in the esteem and practice of all propriety.

The Master said, "I have not seen a person who loved virtue, or one who hated what was not virtuous. He who loved virtue would esteem nothing above it. He who hated what is not virtuous would practice virtue in such a way that he would not allow anything that is not virtuous to approach his person.

"Is there anyone who is able for a single day to apply his strength to virtue? I have not seen the case in which his strength would be insufficient. Should there possibly exist such a case, I have not seen it."

The Master said, "It is only the truly virtuous man who can love or hate others."

The Master said, "If the will be set on virtue, there will be no practice of evil."

The Master said, "Riches and honors are what men desire, but if they cannot be obtained in the proper way, they should not be held. Poverty and inferiority are what men dislike, but if they cannot be avoided in the proper way, they should not be avoided."

"If a superior man abandon virtue, how can he fulfill the requirements of that name?"

"The superior man does not, even for the space of a single meal, act contrary to virtue. In moments of haste, he cleaves to it. In seasons of danger, he cleaves to it."

$\mathcal{T}$sze-chang asked Confucius about perfect virtue.

Confucius said, "To be able to practice five things everywhere under heaven constitutes perfect virtue."

He begged to ask what they were, and was told, "Gravity, generosity of soul, sincerity, earnestness, and kindness. If you are grave, you will not be treated with disrespect. If you are generous, you will win all. If you are sincere, people will put their trust in you. If you are earnest, you will accomplish much. If you are kind, this will enable you to employ the services of others."

*Y*en Yuan asked about perfect virtue.

The Master said, "To subdue one's self and return to propriety is perfect virtue. If a man can for one day subdue himself and return to propriety, all under heaven will ascribe perfect virtue to him. Is the promotion of perfect virtue from a man himself or is it from others?"

Yen Yuan said, "I beg to ask the steps of that process."

The Master said, "Look not at what is contrary to propriety; listen not to what is contrary to propriety; speak not to what is contrary to propriety; make no movement which is contrary to propriety."

Yen Yuan then said, "Though I am deficient in intelligence and vigor, I will make it my business to practice this lesson."

Chung-kung asked about perfect virtue.

The Master said, "It is, when you go abroad, to behave to everyone as if you were receiving a great guest; to employ the people as if you were assisting at a great sacrifice; not to do to others as you would not wish done to yourself; to have no murmuring against you in the country, and none in the family."

Chung-kung said, "Though I am deficient in intelligence and vigor, I will make it my business to practice this lesson."

Sze-ma Niu asked about perfect virtue.

The Master said, "The man of perfect virtue is cautious and slow in his speech."

"Cautious and slow in his speech!" said Niu, "Is this what is meant by perfect virtue?"

The Master said, "When a man feels the difficulty of doing, can he be other than cautious and slow in speaking?"

Fan Ch'ih asked about perfect virtue.

The Master said, "It is, in retirement, to be sedately grave; in the management of business, to be reverently attentive; in intercourse with others, to be strictly sincere. Though a man go among rude, uncultivated people, these qualities may not be neglected."

The Master said, "Artful words and an ingratiating appearance are seldom associated with virtue."

Tsze-chang having asked how virtue was to be exalted, and delusions to be discovered, the Master said, "Hold faithfulness and sincerity as first principles, and move continually to what is right: this is the way to exalt one's virtue."

*H*sien asked what is shameful.

*T*he Master said, "When good government prevails in a State, to be thinking only of salary; and when bad government prevails, to be thinking, in the same way, only of salary — this is shameful.

"When the love of superiority, boasting, resentments, and covetousness are repressed, this may be deemed perfect virtue."

The Master said, "This may be regarded as the achievement of what is difficult. But I do not know that it is to be deemed perfect virtue."

The Master said, "The scholar who cherishes the love of comfort is not fit to be deemed a scholar."

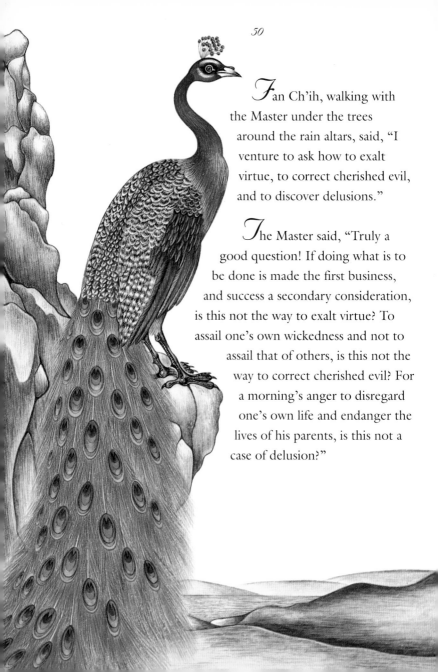

*F*an Ch'ih, walking with the Master under the trees around the rain altars, said, "I venture to ask how to exalt virtue, to correct cherished evil, and to discover delusions."

*T*he Master said, "Truly a good question! If doing what is to be done is made the first business, and success a secondary consideration, is this not the way to exalt virtue? To assail one's own wickedness and not to assail that of others, is this not the way to correct cherished evil? For a morning's anger to disregard one's own life and endanger the lives of his parents, is this not a case of delusion?"

Tsze-kung asked about the practice of virtue.

The Master said, "The mechanic who wishes to do his work well must first sharpen his tools. When you are living in any State, take service with the most worthy among its great officers, and make friends of the most virtuous among its scholars."

The Master said, "The superior man is modest in his speech but exceeds in his actions."

The Master said, "The way of the superior man is threefold, but I am not equal to it. Virtuous, he is free from anxieties; wise, he is free from perplexities; bold, he is free from fear."

The Master said, "When a man can be spoken to, not to speak to him is to waste the man. When a man cannot be spoken with, to speak to him is to waste our words. The wise err neither in regard to their man nor to their words."

$\mathcal{T}$he Master said, "The determined scholar and the man of virtue will not seek to live at the expense of injuring their virtue. They will even sacrifice their lives to preserve their virtue complete."

The Master said, "It is benevolence which constitutes the excellence of a neighborhood. If a man selecting a residence does not fix on one where benevolence prevails, how can he be wise?"

The Master said, "Those who are without benevolence cannot abide either in hardship and poverty or in easy circumstances. The benevolent rest in benevolence; the wise desire benevolence."

The Master said, "The reason why the ancients did not give utterance to their words was that they feared lest their actions should not come up to them."

The Master said, "The cautious seldom err."

The Master said, "The superior man wishes to be slow in his speech and earnest in his conduct."

The Master said, "Virtue is not left to stand alone. He who practices it will have neighbors."

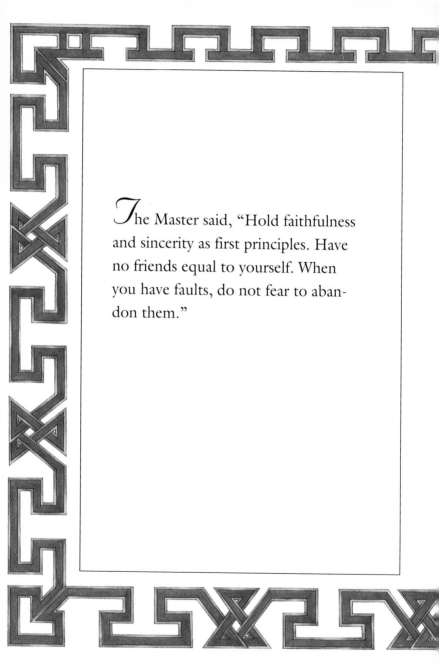

The Master said, "Hold faithfulness and sincerity as first principles. Have no friends equal to yourself. When you have faults, do not fear to abandon them."

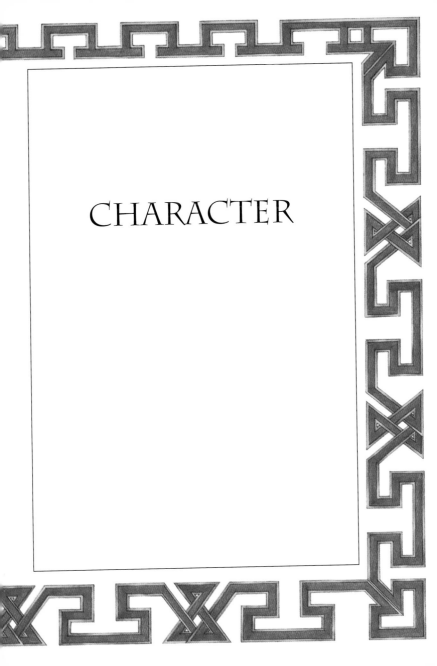

CHARACTER

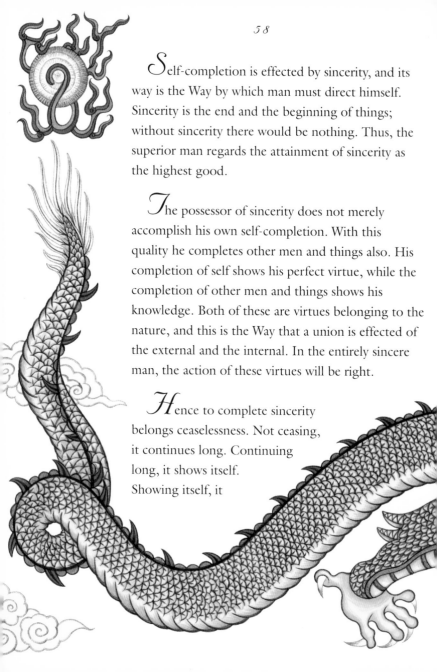

Self-completion is effected by sincerity, and its way is the Way by which man must direct himself. Sincerity is the end and the beginning of things; without sincerity there would be nothing. Thus, the superior man regards the attainment of sincerity as the highest good.

The possessor of sincerity does not merely accomplish his own self-completion. With this quality he completes other men and things also. His completion of self shows his perfect virtue, while the completion of other men and things shows his knowledge. Both of these are virtues belonging to the nature, and this is the Way that a union is effected of the external and the internal. In the entirely sincere man, the action of these virtues will be right.

Hence to complete sincerity belongs ceaselessness. Not ceasing, it continues long. Continuing long, it shows itself. Showing itself, it

reaches far. Reaching far, it becomes large and substantial. Large and substantial, it becomes high and brilliant.

*L*arge and substantial, it contains all things. High and brilliant, it overspreads all things. Reaching far and continuing long, it perfects all things.

*S*o large and substantial, the individual possessing it is the co-equal of Earth. So high and brilliant, it makes him the co-equal of Heaven. So far-reaching and long-continuing, it makes him infinite.

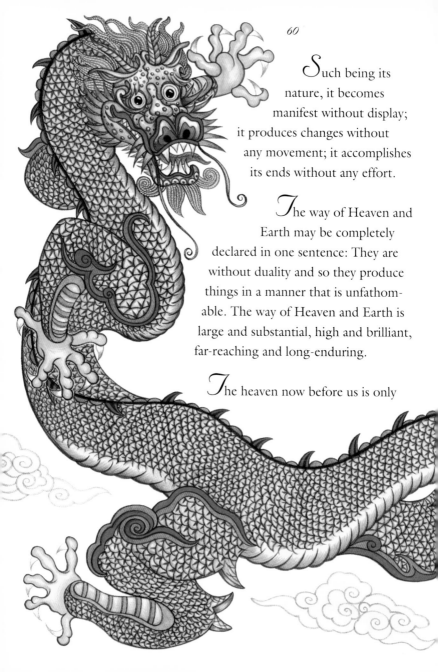

Such being its
nature, it becomes
manifest without display;
it produces changes without
any movement; it accomplishes
its ends without any effort.

The way of Heaven and
Earth may be completely
declared in one sentence: They are
without duality and so they produce
things in a manner that is unfathomable. The way of Heaven and Earth is
large and substantial, high and brilliant,
far-reaching and long-enduring.

The heaven now before us is only

this bright shining spot, but when viewed in its inexhaustible extent, the sun, moon, stars, and constellations of the zodiac are suspended in it, and all things are overspread in it. The earth before us is but a handful of soil, but when regarded in its breadth and thickness, it sustains mountains without feeling their weight and contains the rivers and seas without their leaking away. The mountain now before us appears only a stone, but when contemplated in all the vastness of its size, we see how the grass and trees are produced on it, and birds and beasts dwell on it, and precious things which men treasure are found on it. The water now before us appears but a ladleful, yet extending our view to its unfathomable depths, the largest tortoises, iguanas, dragons, fishes, and turtles are produced in them, articles of value and sources of wealth abound in them.

*I*t is only he who is possessed of the most complete sincerity that can exist under heaven who can fully develop his nature. Able to develop his nature fully, he can develop the nature of other men. Able to develop the nature of other men, he can develop the natures of animals and things fully. Able to develop the natures of creatures and things, he can assist the transforming and nourishing powers of Heaven and Earth, and he may with Heaven and Earth form a trinity.

Next in order is he who cultivates to the utmost the shoots of goodness in him. From those he can attain to the possession of sincerity. This sincerity becomes apparent and, from being apparent, it becomes manifest. From being manifest, it becomes brilliant. Brilliant, it affects others, and, affecting others, they are changed by it. Changed by it, they are transformed.

Only he possessed of the most complete sincerity that can exist under heaven can transform.

*S*ze-ma Niu asked about the superior man.

The Master said, "The superior man has neither anxiety nor fear."

"Being without anxiety or fear, does this constitute what we call the superior man?" said Niu.

The Master said, "When he looks inside and discovers nothing wrong, what is there to be anxious about, what is there to fear?"

Sze-ma Niu, full of anxiety, said, "Other men all have their brothers. I alone do not."

Tsze-hsia said to him, "There is the following saying which I have heard: 'Death and life have their determined appointment; riches and honors depend upon Heaven.'

"Let the superior man never fail to order his own conduct with reverence, be respectful to others and observant of propriety, then all within the four seas will be his brothers. What need has the superior man to worry because he has no brothers?"

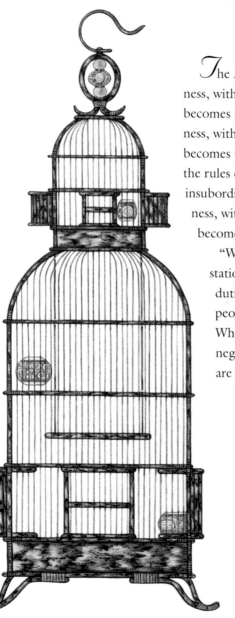

The Master said, "Respectful-ness, without the rules of propriety, becomes laborious bustle; careful-ness, without the rules of propriety, becomes timidity; boldness, without the rules of propriety, becomes insubordination; straightforward-ness, without the rules of propriety, becomes rudeness.

"When those who are in high station perform well all their duties in their relations, the people are aroused to virtue. When old friends are not neglected by them, the people are preserved from meanness."

The Master said, "If a man in the morning is told the Way, he may die in the evening without regret."

The Master said, "A scholar, whose mind is set on truth and who is ashamed of bad clothes and bad food, is not fit to be discoursed with."

The Master said, "The superior man in the world does not set his mind either for anything or against anything; he will follow what is right."

The Master said, "The superior man thinks of virtue; the small man thinks of comfort. The superior man thinks of the sanctions of law; the small man thinks of the favors which he may receive."

The Master said, "There are cases in which the blade springs, but the plant does not go on to flower! There are cases where it flowers, but bears no fruit."

The Master said, "A youth is to be regarded with respect. How do we know that his future will not be equal to our present? If he reach the age of forty or fifty without distinction, then indeed he will not be worth being regarded with respect."

The Master said, "Can men refuse to assent to the words of strict admonition? But what is valuable is reforming the conduct because of them. Can men refuse to be pleased with gentle words of advice? But what is valuable is unfolding their aim. If a man is pleased with these words but does not unfold their aim, and assents to them but does not reform his conduct, I can really do nothing with him."

The Master said, "Hear much and put aside that which you doubt; at the same time, speak cautiously of others and you will afford few occasions for blame. See much and put aside the things which seem perilous; at the same time, be cautious in carrying the others into practice and you will have few occasions for repentance. When one gives few occasions for blame in his words and few occasions for repentance in his conduct, reward will come to him without effort."

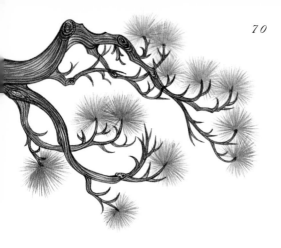

Confucius said, "There are three friendships which are beneficial and three which are injurious. Friendship with the upright; friendship with the sincere; and friendship with the man of much observation: these are beneficial. Friendship with the man of specious airs; friendship with the ingratiatingly soft; and friendship with the glib-tongued: these are injurious."

Confucius said, "There are three things men find enjoyment in which are beneficial, and three things they find enjoyment in which are injurious. To find enjoyment in the discriminating study of ceremonies and music; to find enjoyment in speaking of the goodness of others; to find enjoyment in having many worthy friends: these are beneficial. To find enjoyment in extravagant pleasures; to find enjoyment in idleness and sauntering; to find enjoyment in the pleasures of feasting: these are injurious."

Confucius said, "Those who stand before a man of virtue and station are liable to three errors. They may speak before being spoken to; this is called rashness. They may not speak when spoken to; this is called concealment. They may speak without looking at the countenance of their superior; this is called blindness."

Confucius said, "There are three things which the superior man guards against. In youth, when the physical powers are not yet settled, he guards against lust. When he is strong and the physical powers are full of vigor, he guards against quarrelsomeness. When he is old and the animal powers are decayed, he guards against covetousness."

Confucius says, "There are three things of which the superior man stands in awe. He stands in awe of the ordinances of Heaven. He stands in awe of great men. He stands in awe of the words of the sages.

"The inferior man does not know the ordinances of Heaven and consequently does not stand in awe of them. He is disrespectful to great men. He makes sport of the words of sages."

The Master said, "The superior man is affable but not adulatory; the inferior man is adulatory but not affable."

Tsze-kung asked, saying, "What do you say of a man who is loved by all the people of his neighborhood?"

The Master replied, "We may not for that reason approve of him."

"And what do you say of him who is hated by all the people of his neighborhood?"

The Master said, "We may not for that reason conclude that he is bad. It would be best if those who are good in the neighborhood love him, and those who are bad hate him."

The Master said, "The superior man is easy to serve and difficult to please. If you try to please him in any way which is not accordant with right, he will not be pleased. But in his employment of men, he uses them according to their capacity. The inferior man is difficult to serve, and easy to please. If you try to please him, though it be in a way which is not accordant with right, he may be pleased. But in his employment of men, he wishes them to be equal in everything."

The Master said, "The superior man has a dignified ease without pride. The inferior man has pride without a dignified ease."

The Master said, "The firm, the enduring, the simple, and the modest are near to virtue."

*T*sze-kung asked, saying, "Is there one word which may serve as a rule of practice for all one's life?"

*T*he Master said, "Is not *reciprocity* such a word? What you do not want done to yourself, do not do to others."

*T*he Master said, "In my dealings with men, whose evil do I blame, whose goodness do I praise, beyond what is proper? If I do sometimes exceed in praise, there must be ground for it in my examination of the individual."

*T*sze-lu said, "Does the superior man esteem valor?"

*T*he Master said, "The superior man holds righteousness to be of the highest importance. A man in a superior situation, having valor without righteousness, will be guilty of insubordination; one of the lower people, having valor without righteousness, will commit robbery."

*T*sze-kung said, "Has the superior man his hatred also?"

*T*he Master said, "He has his hatreds. He hates those who proclaim the evil of others. He hates the man who, being in a low station, slanders his superiors. He hates those who have valor merely and are unobservant of propriety. He hates those who are forward and determined and, at the same time, of contracted understanding."

The Master said, "When I walk along with two others, they may serve me as my teachers. I will select their good qualities and follow them, their bad qualities and avoid them."

The Master said, "Heaven produced the virtue that is in me. Hwan T'ui — what can he do to me?"

The Master said, "Do you think, my disciples, that I have any concealments? I conceal nothing from you. There is nothing which I do that is not shown to you, my disciples — that is my way."

There were four things which the Master taught: letters, ethics, perseverance, and truthfulness.

CONDUCT

The Master said, "Is it not pleasant to learn with a constant perseverance and application? Is it not a joy to have friends coming from afar? Is he not a man of complete virtue who feels no offense though men take no note of him?"

The philosopher Yu said, "They are few who, being filial in their obedience, offend their superiors. There have been none who, disinclined to offend their superiors, have stirred up rebellion. The superior man bends his attention to the roots, and, those roots established, all practical courses grow up naturally. Filial piety and fraternal obedience: are they not the root of a man's character?"

The Master said, "Artful words and an ingratiating appearance are seldom associated with true virtue."

The philosopher Tsang said, "I daily examine myself on three points. Whether in transacting business for others I have done my best. Whether in dealing with friends I have been sincere. Whether I have mastered and practiced the instructions of my teacher."

The Master said, "To rule a country of a thousand chariots, duty must be adhered to with reverence and sincerity; there must be economy in spending and love for men; there must be the employment of the people at the proper seasons."

The Master said, "A youth should be a good son at home and respectful toward his elders abroad. He should be earnest and truthful. He should overflow in love for all and cultivate the friendship of the good. If, after the performance of these things, he has time and opportunity, he should engage in studies."

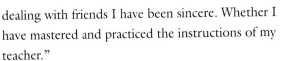

The Master said, "He who requires much from himself and little from others will keep himself from being the object of resentment."

The Master said, "When a man is not in the habit of saying, 'What shall I think of this? What shall I think of this?,' I can indeed do nothing with him."

The Master said, "When a number of people are together for a whole day without their conversation turning to righteousness, and when they are fond of carrying out petty suggestions, theirs indeed is a bad case."

The Master said, "The superior man in everything considers righteousness to be essential. He performs it according to the rules of propriety. He brings it forth in humility. He completes it in sincerity. This indeed is a superior man."

The Master said, "The superior man is distressed by his want of ability. He is not distressed by men's not recognizing him."

The Master said, "The superior man dislikes the thought of his name not being mentioned after his death."

The Master said, "What the superior man seeks is in himself. What the inferior man seeks is in others."

The Master said, "The superior man is dignified, but does not wrangle. He is sociable, but not a partisan."

The Master said, "The superior man does not promote a man simply on account of his words, nor does he reject good words because of the man."

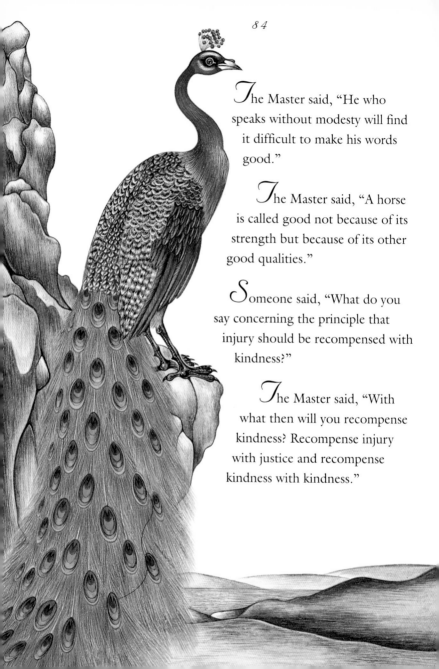

The Master said, "He who speaks without modesty will find it difficult to make his words good."

The Master said, "A horse is called good not because of its strength but because of its other good qualities."

Someone said, "What do you say concerning the principle that injury should be recompensed with kindness?"

The Master said, "With what then will you recompense kindness? Recompense injury with justice and recompense kindness with kindness."

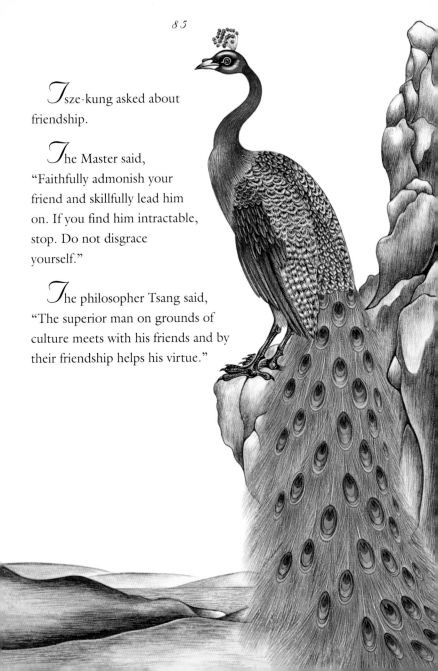

*T*sze-kung asked about friendship.

*T*he Master said, "Faithfully admonish your friend and skillfully lead him on. If you find him intractable, stop. Do not disgrace yourself."

*T*he philosopher Tsang said, "The superior man on grounds of culture meets with his friends and by their friendship helps his virtue."

The Master said, "He who exercises government by means of his virtue may be compared to the pole star to which all the stars turn and which keeps its place."

The Master said, "In the Book of Poetry are three hundred pieces, but the meaning of them all may be embraced in one sentence: 'Do not swerve from the right path.'"

The Master said, "If the people are led by edicts and adherence enforced by punishments, they

will try to avoid the punishment but they will have no sense of shame. If they are led by virtue and adherence is accomplished by the rules of propriety, they will have the sense of shame and will reform themselves."

The Master said, "At fifteen, I had my mind bent on learning. At thirty, I stood firm. At forty, I had no doubts. At fifty, I knew the decrees of Heaven. At sixty, my ear was an obedient organ for the reception of truth. At seventy, I could follow what my heart desired without transgressing what was right."

*T*sze-chang asked Confucius, saying, "In what way should a person in authority act in order that he may conduct government properly?"

The Master replied, "Let him honor the five excellent practices, and banish away the four bad practices and then may he conduct government properly."

Tsze-chang said, "What is meant by the five excellent practices?'

The Master said, "When the person in authority is beneficent without great expenditure; when he lays tasks on the people without their complaining; when he pursues what he desires without greed; when maintains a dignified ease without pride; when he is majestic without being fierce."

Tsze-chang said, "What is meant by being beneficent without great expenditure?"

The Master replied, "When the person in authority makes the things from which the people naturally derive benefit more beneficial; is not this being beneficent without great expenditure? When he chooses the labors which are proper and makes the people labor, who will complain? When his desires are set on benevolent government and he secures it, who will accuse him of greed? Whether he has to do with many people or few, or with things great or small, he does not dare to indicate any disrespect; is this not to maintain a dignified ease without any pride? He adjusts his clothes and cap, and throws a dignity into his looks so that, thus dignified, he is looked at with awe: is this not to be majestic without being fierce?"

Tsze-chang then asked, "What are meant by the four bad practices?"

The Master said, "To put the people to death without having reformed them: this is called cruelty. To require from them suddenly the full scale of work without having given them warning: this is called oppression. To issue orders as if without urgency at first and, when the time comes, to insist on them with severity: this is called injury. And, generally, in giving pay or rewards to men, to do it in a stingy way: this is called acting the part of a mere official."

The Master said, "Without recognizing the ordinances of Heaven, it is impossible to be a superior man. Without an acquaintance with the rules of Propriety, it is impossible for the character to be established. Without knowing the force of words, it is impossible to know men."

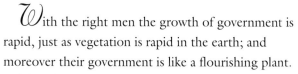

ith the right men the growth of government is rapid, just as vegetation is rapid in the earth; and moreover their government is like a flourishing plant.

Therefore the administration of government lies in getting proper men. Such men are to be got by means of the ruler's own character, which is cultivated by his treading the Way. And the cultivation of the Way is achieved by the cherishing of benevolence.

Benevolence is the characteristic element of humanity, and the great exercise of it is in loving relatives. Righteousness is the accordance of actions with what is right, and the great exercise of it is in honoring the worthy. The degrees of love due to relatives and steps in the honor due to the worthy are produced by the principles of propriety.

When those in inferior situations do not possess the confidence of their superiors, they cannot retain the government of the people.

Hence the sovereign may not neglect the cultivation of his own character. Wishing to cultivate his own character, he may not neglect to serve his parents. In order to serve his parents, he may not neglect to acquire a knowledge of men. In order to know men, he may not dispense with a knowledge of Heaven.

The duties of universal obligation are five, and the virtues wherewith they are practiced are three. The duties are those between sovereign and minister, between father and son, between husband and wife, between older brother and younger, and those belonging to the intercourse of friends. Those five are the duties of universal obligation. Knowledge, magnanimity, and energy, these three are virtues universally binding. And the means by which they carry the duties into practice is singleness.

Some are born with the knowledge of those duties; some know them by study; and some acquire the knowledge after a painful feeling of their ignorance. But the knowledge being possessed, it comes to the same thing. Some practice them with a natural ease; some from a desire for their advantages; and some by strenuous effort. But the achievement being made, it comes to the same thing.

*T*he Master said, "To live in obscurity and yet practice wonders in order to be mentioned with honor in future ages, this is what I do not do.

"The good man tries to proceed according to the Way but when he has gone halfway, he abandons it. I am not able to stop.

"The superior man accords with the course of the Mean. Though he may be all unknown, unregarded by the world, he feels no regret. It is only the sage who can do this."

The Way which the superior man pursues reaches wide and far, and yet is secret. Common men and women, however ignorant, may intermeddle with the knowledge of it, yet in its

utmost reaches, there is that
which even the sage does not
know. Common men and women,
however much below the ordinary
standard of character, can carry it
into practice; yet in its utmost
reaches, there is that which even
the sage is not able to carry into
practice. Great as heaven and
earth are, men still find some
things in them with which to be
dissatisfied. Thus it is that were
the superior man to speak of the
Way in all its greatness, nothing in
the world would be found able to
embrace it, and were he to speak
of it in its minuteness, nothing in
the world would be found able to
split it.

$\mathcal{T}$he Master said, "By nature, men are nearly alike; by practice, they get to be wide apart."

$\mathcal{T}$he Master said, "Extravagance leads to insubordination, and parsimony to meanness. It is better to be mean than to be insubordinate."

$\mathcal{T}$he Master said, "The superior man is satisfied and composed; the inferior man is always full of distress."

$\mathcal{T}$he Master was mild and yet dignified; majestic, and yet not fierce; respectful, and yet easy.

Therefore, the superior man cultivates a friendly harmony, without being weak. How firm is he in his energy! He stands erect in the middle, without inclining to either side. How firm is he in his energy! When good principles prevail in the government of his country, he does not change from what he was in retirement. How firm is he in his energy! When bad principles prevail in the country, he maintains his course to death without changing. How firm is he in his energy!

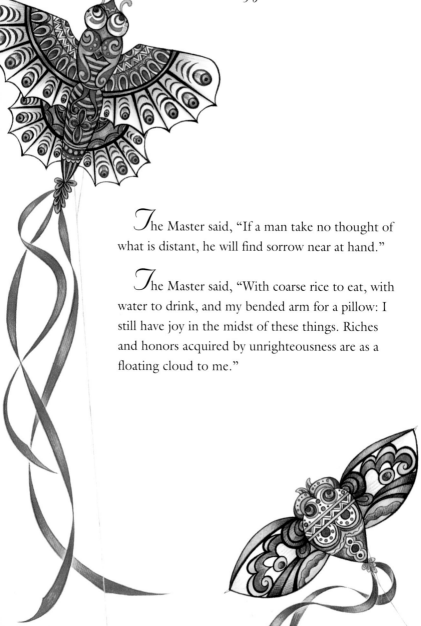

The Master said, "If a man take no thought of what is distant, he will find sorrow near at hand."

The Master said, "With coarse rice to eat, with water to drink, and my bended arm for a pillow: I still have joy in the midst of these things. Riches and honors acquired by unrighteousness are as a floating cloud to me."